I'm Proud of Who I Am
I Hope You Are Too

By: B. Woster

BOOK FOURTEEN

Dedication:

To my family without whose love and support this book would never have been written.

The characters in these books are fictitious. Any similarity to real persons, living or dead, is coincidental and not intended by the author. While the characters are fictitious, the author did use real people as inspiration for her characters' future aspirations. Examples: reporter, poet, occupational therapist.

The places are genuine, as are the facts associated. All are presented with the utmost humility and respect to individuals residing in those countries.

FREE Images obtained from the following sources: istock, freeimages, unsplash, pixabay, pexels, stocksnap, canva, flickr common. This applies to all books in this series.

List of countries featured in BOOK FOURTEEN

Côte d'Ivoire
Ecuador
Iraq
Laos
Latvia
Madagascar
Maryland_USA
Michigan_USA
Missouri_USA
Montana_USA
Nebraska_USA
Nicaragua
Niger
Pakistan
South Africa
Sri Lanka
Tanzania
Uganda
Uzbekistan

Prologue

Have you even once on a clear evening stepped outside or peered from your bedroom window to look up into the night sky, to stare at the stars? I have on many a night. What do I see? I see twinkling lights. You may not see that. You may see the potential of other worlds, or balls of fire, or...nothing wonderous at all. In that we are all very dissimilar. But the fact that we all look at the stars, shows how very much alike we really are.

That is the purpose of this book, to demonstrate that even though we all live in different parts of the world, speak a different language, serve a different god, have different customs, have skin colors that vary in shades from alabaster to deepest brown, and hair color in every hue imaginable...we are more alike than we are different.

We all breathe, eat, drink, live, bleed, and die...and we all have our dreams to which we aspire. We all reach for those stars.

I Am Yacouba

I am from Côte d'Ivoire, which is French for Ivory Coast, and I want to tell you a few things about my home country that I think you might enjoy.

For instance, have you ever enjoyed a cup of hot cocoa? Well, there's a good chance that the beans grown to manufacture that product were right here, in Côte d'Ivoire. That's because we're the largest producers of cocoa beans in the entire world[1]. Do you know the difference between cocoa beans and cacao? Cacao is unroasted, raw, and more bitter while cocoa beans are roasted and tend to be sweeter[2].

But that's not the only thing that Côte d'Ivoire is renowned for. We are also home to the world's largest Christian church: Basilica of Our Lady of Peace in Yamoussoukro. Even though it took four years to build at a cost of around 300 million dollars, it rarely has many people at mass. That's because less than 20 percent of our people are Christian, the rest are Muslim[3].

As for me, I am fifteen years old, and I love all things beautiful. I especially love to paint, but my preferred canvas is people. This is called body art. That's what I want to be one day, but in combination with photography. I say that because I can't see people standing around an art gallery for several hours, after I paint them, to display my work. I would, of course, present the photographed work in the art gallery. Why this? I watched a professional do it when I was visiting London and I knew that's what I wanted to do also.

My name is Yacouba, and I am proud of who I am. I hope you are too.

---

[1] kidadl.com/fun-facts/ivory-coast-fun-facts-history-tourism-culture-and-more
[2] thespruceeats.com/difference-between-cocoa-and-cacao
[3] tripsavvy.com/basilica-of-our-lady-of-peace-1454487

I Am Earlena

Welcome to Ecuador. Our country is named this because the equator runs through it. In fact, we are the only country in the world to be named after a geographical designation.

That isn't the only thing that is unique about my home. Back in 2008, the Ecuadorian government officially granted nature the right of existence, aimed mainly at its rainforests. Nature is no longer viewable as property, rather it has its own constitutional right to exist and procreate. In essence, the law is saying that where life is reproduced and exists, it has the right to regenerate to continue the cycle of life and therefore is protected against anything that may cause its destruction or death[4].

This aligns perfectly with our national symbol, which is a tree. Though we have many beautiful trees in my country, we chose the Cinchona tree as the national symbol for a special reason. It produces quinine, which is used in the cure of malaria[5]. That's important because malaria is nasty. It's a parasite that invades the red bloods cells when mosquitos bite, so finding a cure in a tree was awesome. Maybe that's why our government decided to give them constitutional rights.

As for me, I am now working as a Professional Bridesmaid. I do not stand at the altar with the bride and groom, but I do much of what it takes to make the wedding go well for the bride. Things such as shopping for bridesmaid dresses, updating the gift registry, working with printers on invitations, and many more things that free up the bride to make her day go more smoothly. I am similar to a wedding planner, but I don't help with finding and preparing the wedding venue, nor do anything for the groom. I just help the bride.

My name is Earlena, and I am proud of who I am. I hope you are too.

---

[4] tandfonline.com/doi/abs/10.1080/10455750802575828?journalCode
[5] britannica.com/plant/Cinchona

My name is Farug

and I live in the country of Iraq, which, in Arabic, means 'deeply rooted, well-watered, and fertile'. So many words for such a small country. My country is both very old and very young. We have only been known as Iraq since the early 1920s when it became a nation backed by the British government. Twelve years after that, we gained our independence. Before 1920, we were the Sumerians of Mesopotamia, a civilization dating back over 6000 years, making it the first civilization in this area[6]. It is because of how old our country is that we can claim to have one of the earliest systems of writing. The Sumerian's written language, cuneiform script[7], consisted of differing wedge-shaped marks on clay tablets and was first used around the 31st century BC. Can you imagine if you had to do your homework today scratching shapes into clay tablets? That would take a serious level of dedication.

There is another thing that I will share with you, if you ever decide to visit Iraq, or any other middle eastern country. This is especially important if you are left-handed. You will have to try hard to eat with your right hand, as it is offensive to eat with the left hand[8].

Even though I am only fourteen years old, I am already earning money as a bike messenger for my Uncle's legal firm. I get to carry important documents around the city for clients to sign. I love doing this so much that I plan to open my own bike courier business when I grow up.

My name is Farug, and I am proud of who I am. I hope you are too.

---

[6] khanacademy.org/humanities/world-history/world-history-beginnings/ancient-mesopotamia/a/mesopotamia-article

[7] britannica.com/place-Iraq

[8] muslimaid.org/media-centre/blog/8-surprising-facts-about-iraq/

ello, I am Rathana

Thank you for permitting me to share with you some things about my home country of Laos. For instance, have you ever heard of sticky rice? Well, in my country, it is consumed more than anywhere else in the world. To give you an idea of how much rice we eat, most people in the world eat about two pounds of rice per year. In my country, each person will eat around 340 pounds a year. Because of this we have nicknamed ourselves *luk khao niaow* which means children of sticky rice.

Knowing this, can you guess what work I do here? I work with my family in the paddy fields. Rice is a grain that grows at the tops of grass stalks. The stalks are cut down and thrashed to remove the grains. Baskets are filled and taken to be sold at market. Of course, part of it is kept and cooked at home for us to eat.

Now that I have told you of my people, I will tell you of my country. Here, there is a lake, high in the mountains, called Nong Fa Lake. It is highly respected and feared by our people because the lake is home to a giant snake pig that will consume anyone who dares to enter, so we will not swim or bathe in it[9]. So, if you come to Laos and go to see the lake, please do not jump in.

My name is Rathana, and I am proud of who I am. I hope you are too.

---

[9] 12go.asia/en/laos/interesting-facts

My Name is Abolins

Welcome to my home in Latvia. Have you ever worn a pair of blue jeans? If you have, then you might find it interesting to know that it was actually a Latvian tailor name Jākobs Jufess who invented them. But what made Jufess want to make this type of pants? Well, it just so happened that a customer needed a strong pair of work pants, so Jufess sewed together some duck cloth and reinforced that with copper rivets. That was the first pair of jeans. Levi Strauss comes into the picture because he's the man who gave the money to Jākobs to make them.

Another cool thing about Latvia is that there is a museum solely dedicated to the person we consider to be the world's best liar. His name was Hieronymus Karl Friedrich Freiherr von Münchhausen, and he could tell some really tall tales, such as traveling to the moon. Since he was born in 1720, this is highly improbable. One thing he could never be accused of lying about, however, was his station in life, as he was a Baron. To honor this famed liar, Latvia issues commemorative coins each year, celebrating Münchhausen's birthday[10].

So, I graduated high school last year and just started studying to become an acupuncturist. This is an ancient Chinese remedy for pain and other ailments in which needles are inserted at various nerve centers of the body. Believe it or not, this doesn't hurt, but you might laugh if you catch a glimpse of yourself lying there with needles protruding everywhere, since the needles are left in from five to 30 minutes, depending upon the severity of your ailment or pain.

My name is Abolins, and I am proud of who I am. I hope you are too.

---

[10]thefactfile.org/latvia-facts/

BUNDESREPUBLIK DEUTSCHLAND
20 EURO

Hello, I Am Hery

and I live in Madagascar. Most people have at least heard that name, thanks to the success of the movie with the same name. In the movie though, they had penguins, lions, and zebras, none of which live in Madagascar. Two animals from the movie though specifically live in Madagascar: the Lemur and the Fossa. Interestingly, the Fossa is the Lemurs most feared predator.

My country also has more than 12,000 species of plants that we use to treat all our illnesses with because many people who live outside our capital city of Antananarivo do not have hospitals they can go to. So, herbal remedies are commonplace. Some of our plants, such as the Madagascar periwinkle, are used by people outside of Madagascar because they have been found to help in the fight against diseases such as Leukemia[11].

Now, what can I share with you about myself? I just turned 18 and so I am now working full-time in the cotton fields alongside my dad and mom. We grow cotton to make clothing but also to sell. Cotton is one of my countries main cash crops, so I am happy to be working where I do.

My name is Hery, and I am proud of who I am. I hope you are too.

---

[11] monkeysandmountains.com/madagascar-facts/

# Hi, my name is Mia

I live in the state of Maryland, in the United States, home to the very first public school, which opened in 1635. The Boston Latin School saw such distinguished graduates as Samuel Adams and John Hancock. Even Benjamin Franklin attended but he moved on before graduating.

Most people have heard of Harriet Tubman: the slave who escaped to the north using the Maryland underground railroad, and who took over 300 slaves and indentured servants with her? Well, she was born in Maryland. What made her so brave? Well, she had two children at the time when she heard a rumor that they were planning to sell her to another family. She was scared that she would be separated from her children, so she fled. She later became one of the leading abolitionists in the country[12].

Now I'll share something about me. I start college in the fall to work towards a degree in Electronic Engineering. Ever since I was a kid, I've been fascinated by how things work. Especially elevators and escalators. Those are fun to ride on, aren't they? Anyway, once I get my degree, I'll apprentice with a company to learn to install and maintain both elevators and escalators. This is called an Elevator Mechanic.

My name is Mia, and I am proud of who I am. I hope you are too.

---

[12] jakesmoving.com/10-facts-about-maryland-you-probably-dont-know/

Bank of America
Bank of America

My Name is Barrett

and I am from the great state of Michigan in the United States, which also happens to be home to four of the five great lakes in this region: Lake Superior, Lake Huron, Lake Erie, and Lake Michigan.

Because Michigan is home to so many bodies of water, it should come as no surprise that there are some buildings on a few of them. Still, would you be surprised to know that one of those buildings is a United States Post Office? Well, it isn't there by chance. The vessel J.W. Wescott II delivers mail to crew members stationed on, or freighters passing through, on the Detroit River. Cool!

Michigan is also one of only 13 states that are in more than one time zone. A time zone is an invisible dividing line where the time is the same in each section. There are 24 time zones in the world. So, as I was saying, Michigan is divided...into two time zones. Michigan's upper peninsula has four counties in the central time zone, while the rest of the state is in the eastern time zone. Aside from being in two time zones, we are also home to the least-visited national park. Despite its amazing beauty, Isle Royale National Park is so remote that it has fewer visitors in a year than Yosemite National Park does in a day[13]! Wow!

As for myself, I started working as a model when I was a child, appearing in mostly clothing catalogs. I'm hoping to expand my modeling career, eventually moving into movies. Yep, I want to be an actor.

My name is Barrett, and I am proud of who I am. I hope you are too.

---

[13] nps.gov/isro/index.htm

Hello, I'm Oliviana

and I live in Missouri, which is a state in the U.S. located in the midwest. One of the things we're most famous for is the Gateway Arch in St. Louis. It's so famous because it's the tallest man-made national monument in the United States, standing a whopping 630 feet tall. In 1948, St. Louis held a contest to design a national monument and architect, Eero Saarinen won. Work on his design though didn't begin until 1963. Using todays tools, it may have been built in a few months, but back then it took two years to complete[14].

Moving on from the super interesting to the downright weird, I want to share with you some of the laws that are still on the books today—but I don't think they get enforced anymore. First, bachelor's were charged a $1 tax each year to encourage them to get married; next, it's illegal to hold a yard sale in your front yard in University City; and finally, the weirdest of them all—at least for me—no clawfoot bathtubs can be installed in Kansas City, Missouri, because officials, at the time, were concerned that someone might use actual animals paws as the feet[15].

Now onto me. I graduate next year and it's my goal to become a midwife. Midwives assist in the delivery of babies, but did you know that some have nursing degrees and some do not? I plan to work as a midwife while going to nursing school. That way, when I complete my degree, I'll go from being a DEM (direct-entry midwife) with no degree to a CNM (Certified Nurse-Midwife). I'm excited.

My name is Oliviana, and I am proud of who I am. I hope you are too.

---

[14] gatewayarch.com/experience/about/#our-visitors-have-been-seeing-differently-from-the-very-beginning
[15] linerlaw.com/strangest-laws-in-missouri

My Name is Lucas

I live in the United States in Montana, the only state with a triple divide, a quantum anomaly, and a Yogo. Let me explain since I can imagine the confusion on your faces as you read this.

First, let's start with the triple divide which flows from Triple Divide Peak in the Glacier Mountains. Imagine, if you can, that you pour your water down the sink. It will generally flow along a route and exit at one specific place. If you stand at the top of Triple Divide Peak and do the same thing, the water will immediately split off into three waterways. One path goes straight to the Pacific Ocean and two go off to the Atlantic Ocean via Hudson Bay and the Gulf of Mexico. This could also be called the triple ocean divide[16].

Yogo is a type of sapphire mined specifically in the Yogo Gulch in Montana. What makes it so special is that some of these sapphires, because of the beautiful blue clarity, were used in the Crown Jewels of England[17].

I kept this last bit for last because I freakin' love anything to do with science, which is my favorite subject and why I plan to get my degree in Physics when I grow up. Let me quickly explain what a quantum anomaly is. In super simple terms: it's a force, or energy, that makes things look different than they really are[18]. That's definitely the case with the "Montana Vortex and House of Mystery" in Columbia Falls. That's just one place in case you were wondering. In 1970, the government placed a building around it to help tourists get the most from the vortex. It's best to go with someone so you can see the effects on each other. The vortex is so strong that when you move to one side of the building, you'll look like you shrank six inches. Move to the other side, and you return to normal[19].

My name is Lucas, and I am proud of who I am. I hope you are too.

---

16 openrivers.lib.umn.edu/article/where-the-water-flows-understanding-glaciers-triple-divide-peak/

17 gemgallery.com/yogo-sapphire-gemology

18 accessscience.com/content/quantum-anomalies/757605

19 montanavortex.com/

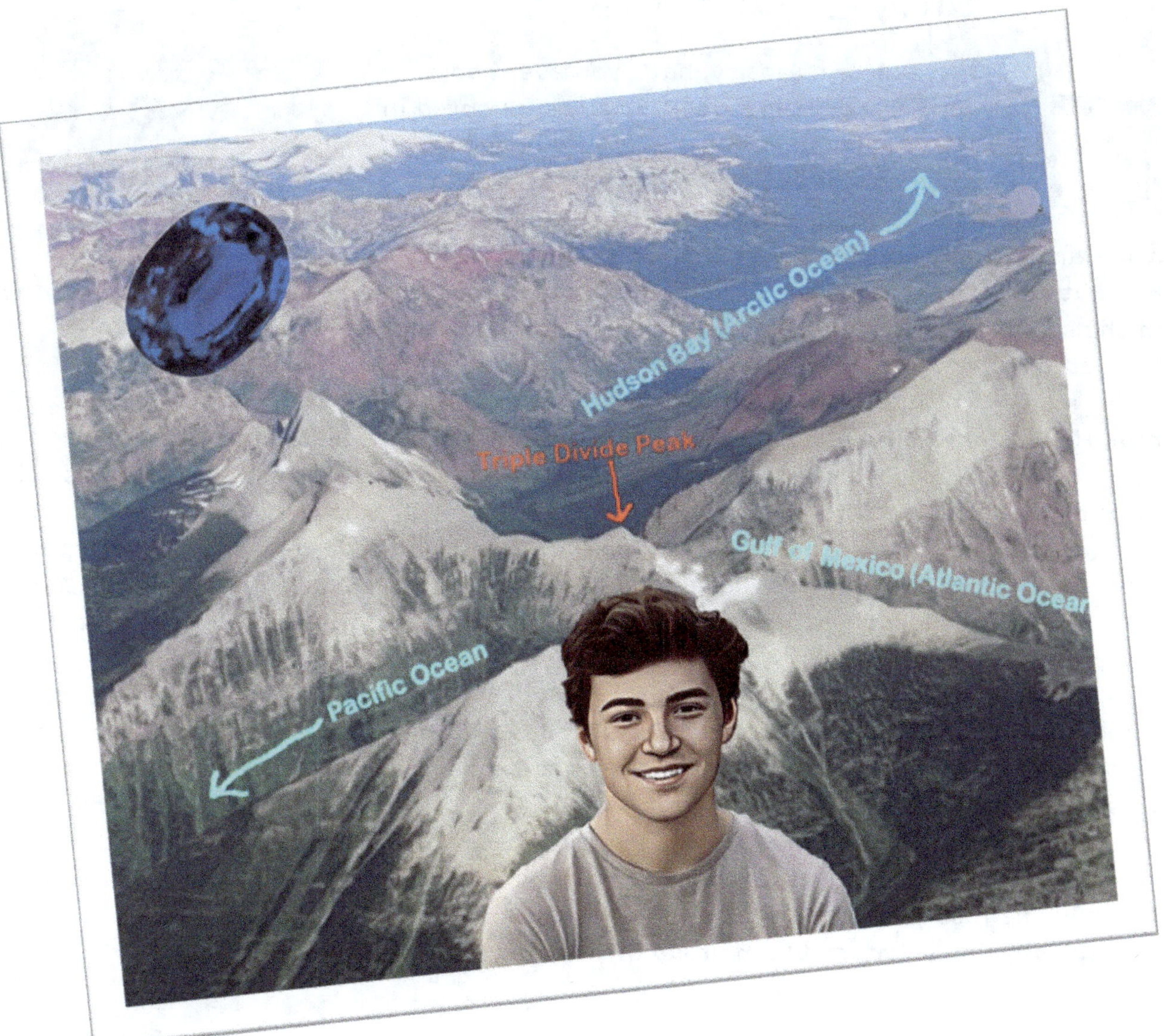

Hudson Bay (Arctic Ocean)
Triple Divide Peak
Gulf of Mexico (Atlantic Ocean)
Pacific Ocean

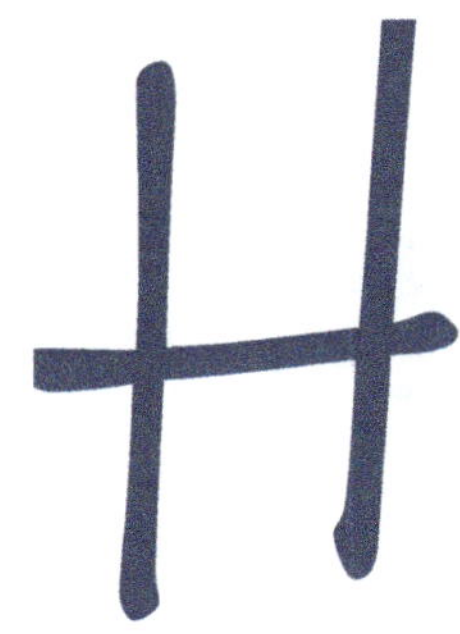ello, I'm Evelyn

Just out of curiosity, have you ever had a glass of Kool-Aid? Well, that was invented in 1927 by Edwin Perkins, who just happened to be born in my home state of Nebraska. What's so interesting about this, to me, is that Perkins initially created a syrup called Fruit Smack, but to make it easier to ship—it got to be really popular—he found a way to remove the liquid from the syrup, turning it into a powder and that's how Kool-Aid was invented[20].

Nebraska has another invention that you may be familiar with: Chef Boyardee. First, let me tell you that Chef Boyardee was a real chef, but his name was actually Chef Boiardi. He was an Italian restaurant owner who changed the spelling of his name so that it would be easier for people to pronounce[21]. Anyway, he wasn't born in Nebraska, nor did he open his first restaurant here, but there is a six-foot-tall statue of Chef Boyardee in Omaha. It was initially placed in front of ConAgra foods who took over the Chef Boyardee brand in the late 1920s. ConAgra moved out of Nebraska in 2015, but the bronze statue remains. It's moved locations many times, but it's still nearby where the ConAgra factory once was[22].

I'm clearly obsessed with food, which is why I have to tell you about "Runza," a fast-food chain that dishes out hot stuffed pastries that are beloved by Nebraskans and, for a long time, were only in Nebraska. They since expanded a bit. 82 locations are in Nebraska, but you'll find a couple in Iowa, Kansas, and Colorado. I must tell you, if you're ever traveling through, you really should stop to get one. They are amazing!

Now, if you haven't guessed what I'm planning to do with my life, I'll give you a hint: it's in the food industry. I plan to become a pastry chef.

My name is Evelyn, and I am proud of who I am. I hope you are too.

---

[20] history.nebraska.gov/publications/kool-aid
[21] foodimentary.com/2012/03/20/a-history-of-chef-boyardee/
[22] roadsideamerica.com/tip/29436

KOOL-AID

I Am Abimael

and I live in the Central American country of Nicaragua, a place that is so tectonically active that we are never wondering if one of our many volcanos will erupt or an earthquake  will occur since the likelihood of both happening is very high. But we don't just face threats from volcanos or earthquakes. Nicaragua is located between the Pacific Ocean—a very volatile body of water—and the Caribbean Sea, so we tend to get battered by hurricanes and tropical storms on a regular basis. If you can get past all of that, my country is a very beautiful place to be.

Still, if you do come to visit, be aware that tourists tend to get confused because we don't have street names or addresses. If you need to go somewhere, you follow landmarks. For example, if you ask someone for directions you may be told to go right at *la iglesias* (church) or left at the local *restaurante* (restaurant) or *parque* (park). So, it isn't that uncommon for someone to get lost—unless you're a resident[23].

Now, I'll share with you my dream, and that is to become a bounty hunter; to hunt down criminals who are trying to escape justice. That is what I want to do. I just finished taking courses on criminal justice to prepare for my new work, which I will be starting this summer. In this, I am very excited.

My name is Abimael, and I am proud of who I am. I hope you are too.

---

[23] worldatlas.com/articles/8-interesting-facts-about-nicaragua.html

I am called Chetachi

Welcome to the country of Niger, the frying pan of the world. Why do you think we are called that? It's because we are one of the hottest nations on the planet. This is probably because we are situated entirely in the southern part of the Sahara Desert. The part closest to the equator, and we all know that the closer to the equator you get, the hotter it gets, so add in desert conditions and you can see why our nickname would be associated with a frying pan.

One of the well-known landmarks in Niger is the Niger River, but what makes it unlike most is that the water is clearer than other rivers in the region. That's because it flows over more rocks, unlike the Nile, and so carries very little sediment along as it moves[24].

Did you know that there was a dinosaur found here back in the early 2000s that is known as the Nigersaurus. Carbon dating determined that this dinosaur roamed the area approximately 110 million years ago. We hear a lot about Brontosaurus or the Tyrannosaurus-rex, but what makes the Nigersaurus so unique is that it had a long, flat head containing up to 500 skinny teeth. Its face is, to me, a cross between a platypus and manatee[25].

That's all I have to share with you today about my country, but I do want to share something about myself. I'm 17 years old now. I just celebrated my birthday yesterday by going paintballing with my friends. That is so much fun to do. Anyway, thinking about all the fun things to do with my friends on my special day made me realize that that's what I want to do for a living—be an event planner. Not just for birthdays though, for any occasion.

My name is Chetachi, and I am proud of who I am. I hope you are too.

---

[24] cs.mcgill.ca/~rwest/wikispeedia/wpcd/wp/n/Niger_River

[25] paulsereno.uchicago.edu/discoveries/nigersaurus/

Hi, I'm Bahija

Welcome to my home of Pakistan. When many people think of my country, they think that it is a hot country, and it is in many places, but there is one place where there are glaciers. In fact, the world's longest glacial system, outside the North or South pole, is in Pakistan, and is located in the Karakoram Mountains[26]. It is two glaciers that combine to make it the biggest: Biafo and Hispar. Together, they are 62 miles long.

I mentioned the Karakoram mountains, so I can also tell you that some of the highest mountains in the world are there. In fact, the second tallest mountain in the world—K2—is here. Did you know, however, that there are other names for this mountain? In Pakistan, we call it Dapsang or Chogori. In English, some people call it Mt. Godwin-Austen, and the Chinese refer to K2 as Qogir Fengin. Either way, I will tell you that it is 28,251 feet high and not one easily climbed. So then why is it called K2? Because it was the 2nd peak measured by explorer Colonel T.G. Montgomerie in 1856 in the Karakoram range. 'K' for Karakoram[27].

Now I will tell you what I get to do for my job. It's so cool. I play video games. No, I'm not a professional gamer, but I am video game tester. I play new video games and then report back to the creators anything that would make it less enjoyable for other players to play. I decided to become a video game tester because I was already spending much of my time on my Playstation, so why not earn a living doing what I already do.

My name is Bahija, and I am proud of who I am. I hope you are too.

---

[26] wikiwand.com/en/Biafo_Glacier
[27] britannica.com/place/K2

ello, I am Bandile

I am 17 years old, and I live in South Africa, where the world's largest-themed resort hotel in the world is located. It's also where I started work this past summer as a doorman. One day, I will work up in the ranks to become the general manager. The resort is called the Palace of the Lost City and surrounding it is over 60 acres of manmade jungle with over two million plants, trees, and shrubs that the guests can meander through at their leisure[28]. It's quite luxurious and is in keeping with South Africa as a nation. What do I mean?

Well, some countries have mainly desert regions, or wetlands, or maybe jungles, but South Africa has it all: deserts, wetlands, grasslands, thick bush, subtropical jungles, and many plateaus. It is truly a land of diversity in nature and was what the resort was trying to recreate.

Thank you for letting me share a bit of my country with you.

My name is Bandile, and I am proud of who I am. I hope you are too.

---

[28] suninternational.com/palace/

Hi, I'm Sanaya

and I want to start by telling you of our sacred mountain, which is called *Sri Pada*, or Adam's Peak in English. To the people of Sri Lanka, my home, there is, on the peak of this mountain, the footprint of Adam, the first man created by God, after he was exiled from Eden. Other people, who come from far and wide, think that it is the footprint of another. The Buddhists say that Buddha left the print when he visited Sri Lanka. Tamil Hindus though believe it was left by Lord Shiva. I do know that when I climb to its peak by candlelight and stand there before the sacred footprint, I am closer to my god[29].

Now that I spoke to you of our sacred mountain, which should be spoken of ahead of food, I will tell you of cinnamon. If you love cinnamon rolls, apple pie, Indian food, or simply appreciate its medicinal uses, then I must tell you that cinnamon came from Sri Lanka. It was discovered millennia ago by the Egyptians who used it in many things: as a spice, perfume, even in embalming. Very versatile is this spice. Even today, nearly all of the world's cinnamon comes from my country[30].

Now I will quickly share with you something about me. I only say 'quickly' because I don't really enjoy speaking about myself. I am 14 years old and it is my hope, one day, to become a world-renowned animator. I am really into Anime, so if I get really good, maybe I can go to work for an animator in Asia. That would be very exciting.

My name is Sanaya, and I am proud of who I am. I hope you are too.

---

[29] buddhanet.net/e-learning/buddhistworld/sri-pada.htm
[30] rickshawtravel.co.uk/blog/10-unique-facts-about-sri-lanka/

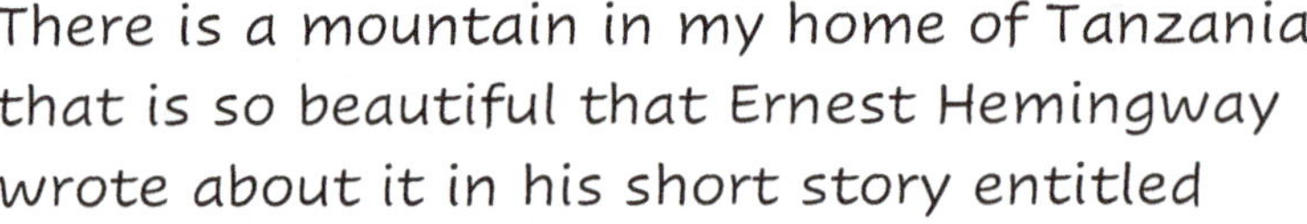ello, I'm Afaafa

There is a mountain in my home of Tanzania that is so beautiful that Ernest Hemingway wrote about it in his short story entitled The Snows of Kilimanjaro[31]. By that title, you probably guessed that I'm speaking of Mount Kilimanjaro. It is only about 19,000 feet high, so tiny compared to mountains like Everest, but it is the tallest in Africa and, since it is not part of a mountain range, it *is* the world's highest single mountain[32].

Another thing in my country that I would love for you to know about is Ngorongoro Crater which is actually a caldera, not a crater. Do you know the difference? A crater happens when a volcano erupts and explodes outward. A caldera is when an eruption causes the volcano to implode or collapse inward. Both of these events create a bowl shape but there is a difference in the way they look. Craters may look more rounded and tend to be much smaller in size, extending to no more than a mile in diameter. Calderas may have parts of their sides missing because of the way the earth slips and slides during the implosion[33]. I just wanted to share that because I think it is one of the most beautiful places I have ever seen, and it was named one of Africa's seven natural wonders[34].

If I could share one thing about what I want to be when I grow up, it would be this. I simply want to be the best person I can be, and to be the best wife to my husband and mother to my children. Just like my mom.

My name is Afaafa, and I am proud of who I am. I hope you are too.

---

[31] en.wikipedia.org/wiki/The_Snows_of_Kilimanjaro_(short_story)

[32] education.nationalgeographic.org/resource/kilimanjaro

[33] education.nationalgeographic.org/resource/types-calderas

[34] andbeyond.com/destinations/africa/tanzania/ngorongoro-crater/

My name is Irumba

Hello from Uganda, where tree planting is required. There are other places where this is true also—that you must plant one tree for every tree chopped down. But in my country, when a tree is harvested, *three* trees must be planted to replace that one. My country started to require this because too many trees were being cut down for homes and firewood and other reasons. It was seriously threatening the homes of our wildlife. That is why it is required now to plant three trees for every one cut down.[35]

Do you know that bananas grow on trees? Do you like them. Well, here in Uganda, we love bananas so much that we use them in many of our foods and drinks. Not just the fruit but also the leaves. *Matooke* is one of my favorite meals to eat. It is made with plantains, a type of banana, and is cooked in banana leaves. Another favorite food is the grasshopper. If you are ever presented with a meal of pan-fried grasshoppers, consider yourself an honored guest.

What I wish to share with you is that I will be getting married next year, but I will not be the one to build my wife her home. She will do that. The only time she will let me work on the house will be when it is time to put on the roof. That is my only responsibility[36] since she will be the one in charge of taking care of that home.

My name is Irumba, and I am proud of who I am. I hope you are too.

---

[35] onetreeplanted.org/products/uganda
[36] answersafrica.com/facts-about-uganda.html

Fried
Grasshoppers

Hi, I am Alisher

and I'm from the country of Uzbekistan. In my country, bread is a sacred part of our meal, so much so that turning a loaf upside down or placing it on the ground will bring you much bad luck. It is also important, if going away for a while, to take a small bite from our Uzbek bread and put it aside to eat upon returning. If going to be gone for a while, then the bread is buried or placed hidden beneath the home until you come back to eat it.

There is also this that I wish to share with you should you come for a visit. This is very important to our people. Uzbek men will greet each other by placing their right hand on their chest. This is usually initiated by the younger man. They may or may not shake hands. Women greet other women by placing their right hand on the left shoulder. If a woman and man meet, the woman will place her hand on her chest and remain at a distance. The men and women of my country often remain distant from each other. It is our custom[37]. In the bigger cities, things are less strict.

As for me, I wish to share with you what my job will be when I graduate from school in another year. I want begin school to become a psychologist, but I do not wish to open a practice with my degree. I want to start an art therapy program instead. This is because I love people and care about their feelings and truly believe that painting or molding clay is a great way to relieve stress. It works for me.

My name is Alisher, and I am proud of who I am. I hope you are too.

*Art therapy image: https://www.pinotspalette.com/naperville/blog/creative-life/pinotspalettenaperville-art-therapy-techniques-to-help-you-de-stress

---

[37] onhisowntrip.com/most-interesting-facts-about-uzbekistan/

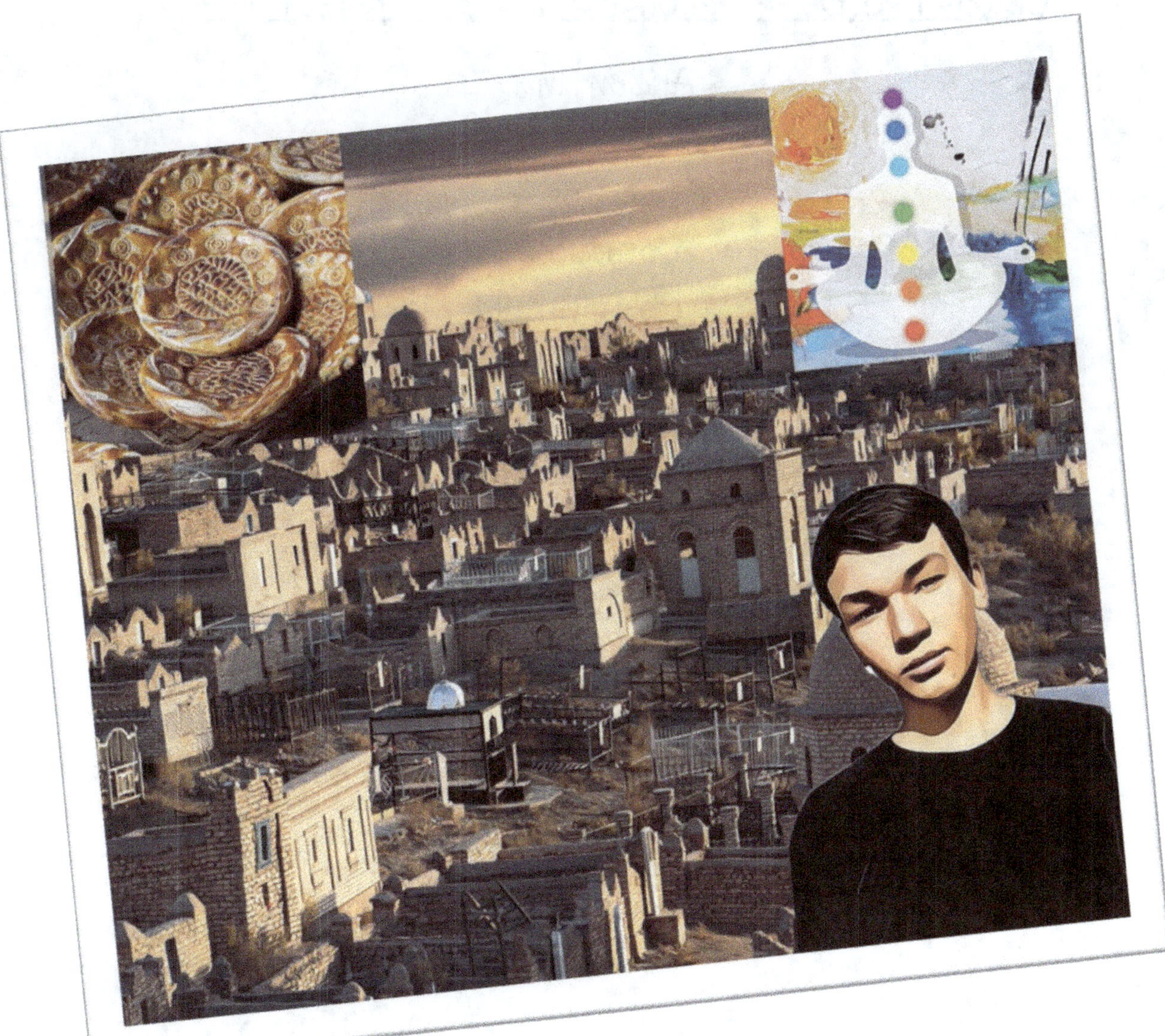

COUNTRIES FEATURED IN BOOK FIFTEEN

Argentina
Australia
Cabo Verde
Comoros
District of Columbia_USA
Northern Mariana Islands
Mozambique
Oman
Saint Vincent and the Grenadines
Shetland Islands
Slovenia
South Carolina_USA
Vietnam
Tahiti
Tennessee_USA
United Arab Emirates

AUTHOR BIO

Barbara Woster is an educator, author, and business owner. She has been writing since the age of twenty-one, but her passion for the written word began when she was fourteen after suffering a broken knee.

After surgery to repair the damage to her knee, Barbara was laid up in bed for nearly a year with not much to do. To relieve the boredom, her mother bought her Harlequin Romance books because they were inexpensive and an easy read for a young girl.

One afternoon, her father came in to check on her and saw all the romance books strewn across the bed, then turned and left the room without a word. He returned shortly after and tossed a book onto her lap. "You need to broaden your reading horizons," he said. He placed a kiss on her cheek then left again. The book was *Iceberg* by Clive Cussler.

From that day forward, Dirk Pitt became her ideal character, and a love for the written word was formed. When she became an adult, she decided that she too wanted to create stories that inspire others to read, write...imagine.

For more information on this author and her books, visit https://barbarawosterauthor.com

www.ingramcontent.com/pod-product-compliance
Lightning Source LLC
Chambersburg PA
CBHW080505030726
47592CB00011B/3261